THE FALLS

First published 2000 by
Worple Press
12 Havelock Road
Tonbridge
Kent TN9 1JE

ISBN 0 953947 3 1

Worple Press is an independent publisher specialising in poetry, art and
alternative titles. It is part of The Worple Company Ltd. (Reg. No.
3829499). **Worple Press** can be contacted at:

12 Havelock Road, Tonbridge, Kent TN9 1JE
Email theworpleco@aol.com
Fax: 01732 352 057

Typeset and printed by Peepal Tree Press

CLIVE WILMER

THE FALLS

worple
press

To Robert Wells

CONTENTS

There is one custom among [the Babylonians] which is wholly shameful: every woman who is a native of the country must once in her life go and sit in the temple of Aphrodite and there give herself to a strange man.... Once a woman has taken her seat she is not allowed to go home until a man has thrown a silver coin into her lap and taken her outside to lie with her. As he throws the coin, the man has to say, 'In the name of the goddess Mylitta' – that being the Syrian name for Aphrodite. The value of the coin is of no consequence; once thrown it becomes sacred, and the law forbids that it should ever be refused. The woman has no privilege of choice – she must go with the first man who throws her the money. When she has lain with him, her duty to the goddess is discharged and she may go home, after which it will be impossible to seduce her by any offer, however large.

Herodotus

[We'll] take upon's the mystery of things
As if we were God's spies

King Lear

I

VISITATION

Who are you that have stepped into the light
      so unforeseeably
        that 'goddess' seems the word?
          how else to name

that beauty more than beauty, inwardness
      so perfectly made flesh
      we are abased by it
        and almost fear

there will be no way back – though to come back,
      the vision thus relinquished,
      is what we least desire?
        I most desire

you here and now, although, till here and now,
      I could not yet have wanted
      what still remained unknown –
        except, we're told,

there'd be no dream of earthly paradise
      without the fallen earth.
      Your body is a thing
        as the earth is

but with the fragrance of another world...
      O gentle girl, who tremble
      when you are touched, whom I
        tremble to touch,

you rend the dark like lightning, leaving day
      solemn with ravage, yet
      bright with the evidence
        of visitation.

THE HERON

The heron nests in the mountains:
she takes to the heights, no bird
can reach as high as she can,
she is not to be touched.

My anxious thought has found
her refuge out, but still
the more you make pursuit,
the more she fends you off.
For me it is enough
to follow her and hold her
in view, for the eye's pleasure.
She is not to be held.

Many have followed her
thinking to take her, yet
whoever finds himself
closest is first forgotten.
What more could a man desire
than but to look on her,
devotion thus repaid?
She is not to be grasped.

I have never seen a creature
so fine, so elegant,
so far beyond possessing.
From her great height she disdains
all men who hope; and therefore,
being so beautiful,
she makes the world her captive.
She, though, will not be caught.

after Juan del Encina

VACATIONS
for M.L.

Look: snow on Helvellyn's peak
at Christmas time. How the cold shines!
 How, stooped by their white burden,
  bare trees sway over hard lakes!

Nothing for it but to heap the blaze
with more logs and, in genial mood,
 bring out your darkest wine,
  its summer heat four winters old.

What brought us here, frost in our hair?
What wrecked your ship? Broke down my roof?
 Let be: before too long,
  seas will be tranquil, trees tall.

As for tomorrow – what it will bring –
put that and regret aside. For now,
 think each new day pure gain –
  just as it is for those whose bloom

is freshly upon them, who can't envision
their own sweetness. Watch them at dusk
 spill out into warm streets
  where jasmine twines with honeysuckle,

then hear, as from a gurgling spring,
the laughing murmurs of a girl
 beyond the streetlamp's arc:
  how she croons *No, no*, without resisting.

after Horace

TO PYRRHA

What skinny lad, sweet-smelling, rubbed with oil,
has got you where he wants you, couched with roses
       down there in your snug nook?
  Is it for him you braid your blond hair

in careless elegance? Poor boy, how often
will he protest at change in fate and women,
       shocked at a sea turned rough
  as the dark winds bear down on it,

though he enjoys you now – thinking you gold
all through, lovely forever, your desires
       forever fixed on him –
  and hears no breeze stirring. For all

who are struck by you untried, it's a grim outlook.
And me? I long ago took out a policy
       that charges a heavy premium
  on shipwrecks and other acts of God.

after Horace

lose what you are
    fear   desire

dark
    made darker still by the white ray:
she turned away from me, as if to bow
to the moon's face, but leaned on the rough sill,
so that her breasts hung softly in my hands

then the flames flared and leapt,
I pushed lightly and the entrance gave

SOFT AND HARD PORN

1. *Artemis*

You turn the page

she steps out
of the bath, she looks
from her long reflection
back at you

humbling you,
those eyes
as of a god

Light answers
from her lips'
red gloss
and from points of
the tumbling
hair her left arm's
raised to hold up

So that you note
the trenched sweep of
the spine, so elegant,
the fruit-round rump and
from under the armpit the
weight and sway
of a breast, the nipple unseen

except in the mirror
beneath
that baleful stare

2. Persephone

          dark interior
the opening pierced with gems

          bright
against that setting of
            spread lips

it begins here   the feeling journey

          hers
a nomad privacy
            framed
all her wealth displayed

A VISION

"In a doorway, I swear.
            There were these two –
I was late cycling home
            a gorgeous night
midsummer and people
            out partying still.
I freewheeled past this shop
            they were necking there
but she had her breasts out
            one hand on his fly.
The bike sailed breezily on –
            I did a sort of
drawn-out double-take,
            turned back up the hill
and there she was
            on her knees now
blowing his horn.
            Imagine
how I felt:
            like some Sicilian peasant
hailed one day
            by an angel on the dung-heap –
or this girl walking ahead
            in a blue scarf
turns to accost him, he stares
            and it's the Virgin.
They're funny, Catholics: so
            literal sometimes
about the things of the spirit,
            even fleshly."

FIN DE SIECLE
Montmartre, 1890s

Don't look, but the sun is setting and the leaves
Out there on the silver birches have turned gold:
You can almost *hear* them, jangling in the wind!
Why not paint that? Oh but you see, I do –
Searching your curves and hollows, yet with this
Decay staining the atmosphere, this chill,
This fog in the soul's crevices.

And then, you know, I regard you with desire,
Which is the desire of art, and that includes
The desire for it to end, for you to leave
And for the night to come.
                              Well, shall I go
To *The Green Monkey* for the *décolletage*
Of that girl who hangs around there, the gas light
Finding a coarser gold between her breasts
As it burns lips and cheeks a fiercer red?
Or to the gilded dark of *Sacré Coeur*
Where I can light a candle and attend
To the drone of Vespers, conscious that outside
The last rays yield crushed russet to grey ash?

But that's already to have gone too far.
I like this moment, now:
This is the time when, work my compelling passion,
I nonetheless start longing. For what else?
Not to stop work but for something to be there
When the work stops. Moments, by definition,
End – without ending there can be no meaning,
No picture without frame.

So here, your chemise, your stockings, and all that –
Just let me wash this brush. Thank you, I share
Your pleasure in it. Though I have you here,
It's always inward too, an act of mind –
Just knowing how you look
Where you're not seen, watching the light pass
And labouring to catch one moment of it
To make your moment, charged with other times.

As for me, what I've been working for
Comes when you've left, although it couldn't come
If you had not been here. My muffler on,
I'll saunter down to watch the afterglow
Beyond the cemetery, as way beneath
Paris puts on her evening dress, her jewels
Flickering more acutely for the dark.

THE NEW ERA
A lake near Dresden, 1910

In the *New Era* coffee-house, that's where.
Reinhard was with you, and he came across
To interrupt my reading. You can't, I think,
Have noticed me: by then you were too deep
In conversation with — what *is* her name? —
Your flirty friend. But me, once I had seen you,
I couldn't keep my eyes off. I can't now.
Which is as well in one who's painting you —
More lovely here in the pure light of day
Than in the gaslamp's aura; though for me
As I paint now, the sun being so intense,
You struggle with the shadows and I fight
To guard you from those stark contrastive schemes
That coarsen. As I say, later that night,
Dear Reinhard took you home and, in a sort
Of trance, I followed, keeping to the dark.
I mooned around outside your house until
The lights went out. It was then that everything
Inside me, like a forest of dry shrubs,
Caught fire and the flames leapt from branch to branch
Till I was white with heat.
To cool the blaze
I set out walking, dawn my only goal,
And with no thought of them I came upon
The ladies of the night, there on the *Platz*,
Hugging the streetlamps in their fissured clouds
Of smoke and frosted breath.
No, dearest, no,
It wasn't that but, rather, up till then
What had I painted but those mournful girls,
Hair down in dark cascades, and brooding knights,

Their chainmail meshed with thorny briars, each rose
Impeccably itself? These were real.
They were everything I had not yet touched.
They strutted like exotic birds – bright plumage
And faces brighter than my palette is
That spoke to me of my work.
Therefore it seems
They and not Reinhard brought me to these dunes
Here by the lake where this your nakedness
Is pure and paradisal, so that Adam
Can roam again among the clumps of growth,
Now free to sample. Yes, we will have change.
I'll give what we can see these wilder hues –
Gold flesh on purple waves with crimson sky –
And draw a blueprint for the time to come.
We are making a new world.

II

IN MEMORY OF GRAHAM DAVIES, PSYCHOTHERAPIST
(1937 – 1993)

You, invisible, once again, I address.
I almost seem to welcome the distress
That puts me back in touch with you once more.
Remember how I called you 'my old whore'
And how you laughed at that? – for, young or old,
Whores charge for love, even those with hearts of gold.
So you charged and I loved. And though you'd try
To justify the fact, I had to lie
On the same couch where other clients had lain.
Our play was serious, yet it was quite plain
That all the passion in it came from me.
You tricked me out of feeling solitary
By being others for me. That way, you
Were priest as well as healer, teacher too,
And father. My dead father. *You* are dead
They tell me, Graham. This is now my head
We talk in and I cannot turn to reach
The man behind the couch whose flights of speech
Lodged in my own, much as his garden birds
Merged with its foliage. Even now your words
Stay with me: I can hear your sympathy
And irritation, your lucidity
And warmth, your massive knowledge, your quiet laugh...

You had, framed in your hall, a photograph
I loved – it was of the Christ Pantocrator
From Vézelay, sculpted there above the door.
He gazed impassively into the minds
Of all who entered. Lapped by rushing winds,
Harried by turbulence, huge hands aflame,
He sits in judgement there. He is the same
In wrath or love, stern judge or gentle son.

27

His is the tranquil character of stone,
Hard and unmoving, sensuous, warmed by light,
Changeless, yet, suffering the chisel's bite,
Yielding to what it images: the soul.

That was your business.
                        In a different role –
Traveller, pilgrim, call it what you will –
You stare from a snap-shot. You don't look ill
Exactly, but somehow edgy, as you half
Turn from the hands that clinched the photograph
Toward the horizon – anxious to be gone...
At least, so it would seem to anyone
Who knew this was the day before you died.
The camera might have caught you in mid-stride
There by the cliff's edge, making for the sea,
Which, struck by light, almost transcendently
Blurs into sky in one pale silver blaze.
They found you in mid-stride, but with your gaze
Turned inward and your body on the ground
Still plunging out across Iona Sound
Toward the heave of mountain, it would seem,
Vision outpacing sense, Elijah's team
Already harnessed to the chariot-shaft
And pawing the clouds.
                        Where you were photographed
In fact was Staffa, but you went to die,
The next day, on Iona, where the sky
And land seem more akin, I'm told; for there
Beach, field and outcrop are a single layer
Laid thinly on the water, and the land's
Transparent frailty timelessly withstands
The ocean's grim authority. I know
Places like that. In them, the spirit so
Permeates all the common world with thought
They bear the traces of a different sort

Of journey to one's own. Unreconciled
To your departures, I was like a child
Who won't believe his elders quite exist
Outside his orbit. You went south and east
As well as north, but always you returned –
As elders do. When, like a boy who's learned,
I felt the strength to travel on my own,
You stabilised in my thought, settling like stone.
We'd meet at concerts. Do you recall that voice –
A pure soprano, firm yet tenuous –
We heard, in a bare chapel, make lament
Without vibrato or accompaniment
For a crusader love? We followed where
It gave at last on silence and thin air,
Ending as if intended to go on,
Lost in the space it filled.
                                        Where have you gone?
Where have you *all* gone, who are invisible?
Into the world of light? Or have you all
Turned inwards, melting into thought instead?
Or vanished? Graham, when I saw you dead,
And saw my mother dead, you were both mere
Things, as desks and chairs are things, no more
Life in you than in stolid wood that once
Stirred all through with the rich circumstance
Of wind and weather. Yet the leaves still sprout
In the mind's branchings, and tenderly reach out
For light as the birds come, nestle there and stay.
I point to them. You comment. What you say
Is much like what you said, though in this way,
Somehow, you teach me more. I always knew
The richness of the mind, saw how it grew
Through all the human seasons, how it fed
On all the variousness outside the head;
And yet I never could accommodate
Its quirks, its weirder vagaries, the dull hate

29

Its warmest love includes, its sullen sluice
Of loathsome wants, the intermingled juice
Of painfullest secretions, how its strange
Flirtations with the arbitrary derange
And dissipate. Recoiling from that mess,
I looked instead for grace and shapeliness
And luminosity. So how much stranger
It now seems that, today, I feel less danger
From that – having looked into it with you –
Than I could have imagined. Stranger, too,
That the great world seems grander and the mind
Richer, more luminous – thought more refined
By being sieved through talk, more prone to form
For all those crazed departures from the norm.

But in the darkness, when I face your loss
And see my journey as it always was,
Unfinished, thwarted and circuitous,
I doubt the powers I trusted, I resent
The pain, hard cash and energy I spent
On the long quest, I feel the tender scars
Reopen now, and the old tide of fears
Comes in around me… Then, to my surprise,
I find that I am back with you, my eyes
A-birding through your window, and your voice
Lighting on this occasion to rejoice
In requiem – I feel it on my scalp,
A *cantus firmus* which I cannot help
But build on polyphonically, the world
Eluding us as we, with word on word,
Elaborate upon infinity –
Such magnitude, such multiplicity,
So simple. Graham, I first came to you
Unable to believe it quite untrue
That great creating nature was divine.
I am none the wiser. But, now you resign

Your part in that great argument and turn
Half-way away from me, I seem to learn
That, being dead, you *are* what I now know.
So I consult you, hoping that way to grow
A better man, and you so speak to me,
Not from the throne of Vézelay, vertically,
But from the shadows that I leave behind me.
Like them, it is of myself that you remind me –
Though you remain the trusted friend no less,
Whom, though invisible, I again address.

III

EPITAPH

M.A.B.B. (1925-1996)

Why do the robin and the butterfly
Linger where you have lingered? Can they know
The knowledge, wit and charity that lie
Here now and yet go with you where you go?

AT A FRIEND'S FUNERAL

i.m. Michael Bulkley

Parce, Domine, enim nihil sunt dies mei

Spare me, Lord, for my days are nothing.

My friend, though, who is not here as I am,
Is everywhere and in all things.

What is it binds us then?
                              Nothing but words –
This reading, this incantation, this great cry,
These voices woven in polyphony
Unwoven into silence.

Tomorrow, only the words in my head
As my days unpick themselves, till they are nothing.

WOOD WORK

i.m. Henri Gaudier-Brzeska
(1891—1915)

1.

Henri Gaudier

from an enemy
rifle-butt
carved

Caritas
an infant
at each dug

condemned to die

2.

gouge
      into wood grain
against
      gun metal

in tempore belli
    Pax

STONE WORK

Floor tomb, Santa Croce, Florence

Cut in stone,
    coat and hood
fall from him
    in the folds of sleep.

The good mind
    has made its mark
in the pillow,
    a slight impress.

More gradual
    than forgetting is,
steps passing
    efface features.

FERNANDO PESSOA'S LISBON

1. *Flat*

Plain, square, modern, small:
room enough, it would seem,
for the populous brain.

2. *Bar*

Black ink, green liquor:
how the mind
poisons the indivisible flesh.

A BAROQUE CONCERTO

To Edgar Bowers, at 70

'Pure mathematics!' That's what you exclaimed
Across the polite applause to me, enthused
By a forgotten opus hardly famed
In its own time or place. I wasn't used
To seeing you moved and vulnerable: it brought
Another harmony into my head,
The divisions of your verse, its metres taut,
Drawn from the order trusted to the dead.

A love of the abstract... yet you evoke,
Through poignant scenes of Europe sketched in youth,
An order that's the sharper for the smoke;

And, later on, make your locality –
That golden coastline where civility
Encounters nature – witness to the truth.

CASA NATAL DE BORGES

'a man who, in an age that worships the chaotic idols of blood,
earth and passion, preferred... the lucid pleasures of thought
and the secret adventures of order.'

Borges on Valéry

The secret adventures of order
Began in this emblem of the *Belle Epoque*:
The orderly elegance of the *haut-bourgeois*,
Who have secrets but few adventures.

Lost to its old seclusion, smeared with grime,
It endures quotidian rage, an inhuman alarm
And in shop windows intimacies laid bare.
It persists, though,
Like the last, yellowing, undecayed incisor
In a mouth whose gleaming beauty is long gone.

The city as *locus* of civility:
An accident of time perhaps? But time
Moves on and leaves behind it
An invisible city, continuing, made of messages
Strung together by those who have most cherished
The lucid pleasures of thought.

Buenos Aires, 1999

41

W.S. GRAHAM READING

Word drunk they called him. Well:
I don't know about *words*.
                    He sat there turning the pages
unable to fix on a single verse
plaintive and truculent
                    quarrelling with the book,
as if to surrender to a single instance
of language
                    was to surrender.

Then: 'Read any one of them,' somebody cried:
'they're all marvellous!'
                    And we beheld a marvel:
an Archangel
                    a little damaged
igniting the dark firmament with speech.

OLIVIER MESSIAEN

1. Wilderness

What is it this cacophony,
this concord of sounds, some sweet,
some not so sweet? It is
the order of things.

The wingbeat of Bonelli's eagle,
a thunderclap, the song of the hermit thrush,
the city at night – zigzag of siren and horn,
the whoosh of the desert wind.

Terrible is this place: it is
the house of God, the gate of heaven.

2. Cathedral

To read by analogy: columns,
Like tree-trunks, disclose light;
Birds, in the foliate capitals,
Are wide-billed amid fruit

But silent, until *this*
Radiates through it all.
Then the birds sing, the leaves hiss,
Wind shushes, though air is still.

3. Revelation

You who, in what is made of time, end time:
        hatched out of dissonance,
the single, held, unending chord or chime

43

THE FALLS
for Jim Spates

I am haunted by this memory of the falls:
The turbulent water with its bloom of froth
        Hung like a curtain, still
        Changeless and invariable;
Yet spat and spumed, dripped and cascaded, gushed –
Eased itself of the burden the great lakes
        Had urged upon it. Also,
        Viewed from the side, it stood
From the rock wall like a sheer and polished pane
At the top curved and stooping to the plunge –
        To the deep catastrophe
        That shattered it – and then
Rebounded back as star-flung spray, a deathless
Tower of it, rising, as if in worship –

*

Did Jackson Pollock
                    when he painted *One*
know the Lord's beauty by it?
                    What we call
randomness –
                    the white stream
lashed over brown and purple
                    sprayed and flecked –
not at all
                    deep canyons of the underself
but the order in which things fall,
                    or what intelligence will make of them.
Draped from the rock it
                    frills but falls:
the same pattern, never
                    the same water.
You will find
                    (I must tell you)
no great man
                    not a man of law.

                    *

Further downstream we had paused at other falls:
Slight trickles, graceful cataracts, rapids, weirs,
    The still rock around which
    A rope of current tugged
And, frothing from some ledge, a watery fringe
Of tasselled elegance. Each one of them,
    For all the vehement clamour,
    Displayed rule and design;
Though they fell, they fell by the same laws,
And all such law breeds pattern. This one, however,
    Was quite another thing:
    A gulf in the earth's crust,
Chaos to us – ocean or milky way –
And order, therefore, in the larger mind.

*

the sun and the other stars
    the beating heart
        the snow-melt

driven, crying
of this steep place afraid
        the common pass

but fraying there
the vast drum of woven stuff unwinding,
        the dripped lace

no measure fine enough
eye or finger or numerate brain

immutable change
        made and remade
laws finer than any known of men

from things made
    being seen and understood
        the invisible things

each frill and fibre
        eternal power

ACKNOWLEDGEMENTS

Some of these poems have appeared in the following periodicals, to whose editors thanks are due: *Agenda, Critical Quarterly, la fontana, PN Review, Threepenny Review, Times Literary Supplement*. 'Epitaph' has been carved on the gravestone of my late friend Michael Bulkley in Histon Road Cemetery, Cambridge. The epigraph quoted from *The Histories* of Herodotus was translated by the late Aubrey de Sélincourt (Penguin Classics, 1954); I am grateful to my friend Michael Vince for pointing this passage out to me.